A Mint, A Siren, and The Logos

Patrick Blonski

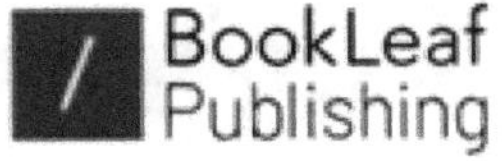

Presentation by *BookLeaf Publishing*

Web: www.bookleafpub.com

E-mail: info@bookleafpub.com

ISBN: 9789357210584

First edition 2022

Dedicated to the lost and wanderers and
especially to my dear friend, Araminta

ACKNOWLEDGEMENT

For the many blessings received from the Queen from Heaven, Her Son, and the communion of saints

Beauty

Just as the moonlight drives
the darkness from the timeless sea
to show its majesty.
So does it reveal the beauty
in that night, through the pearl white light.
To unveil you to my heart.

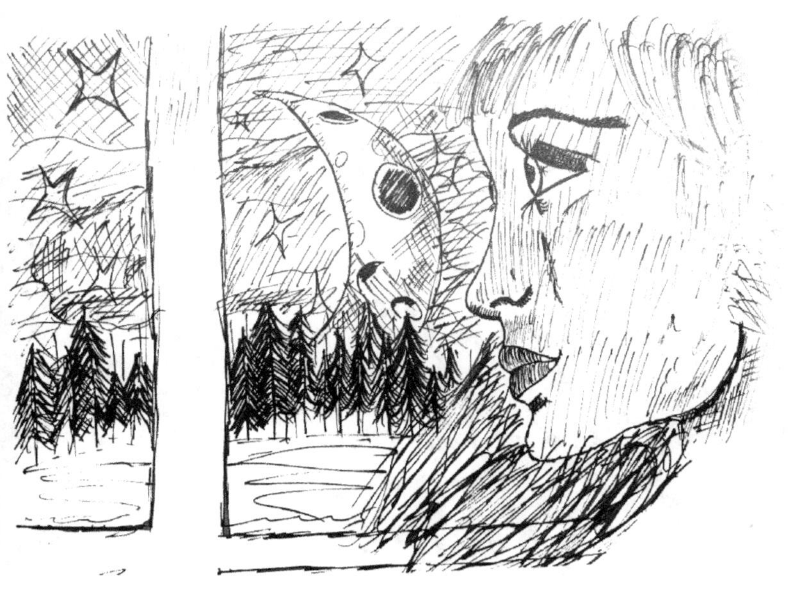

Silence

The silence whispers, its song so faint.
Though the heart still dances to the part.
Blood is flowing, ripples echoing for embrace.

Falling

Don't let go again
I am dancing with my words
I don't want to fall

Death

Blanket, o so soft
comfort me as I doze.
For my journey towards death
is lonely and tiresome, for at best
you prepare me for the eternal rest.
Blanket let the darkness come for me.

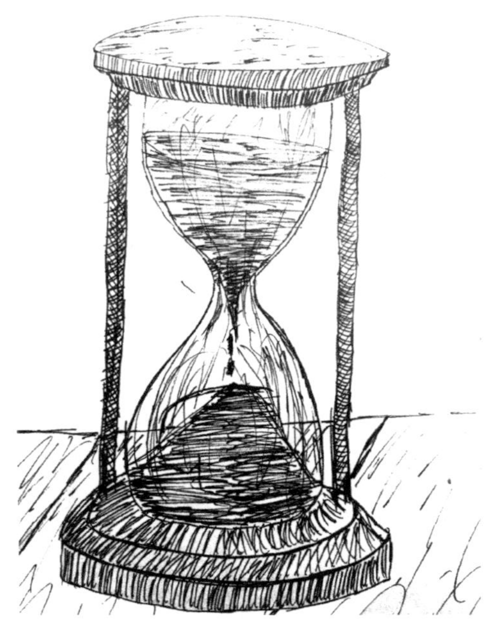

Smile

The darkness of the night has just arrived
the golden glow of the street illuminates your
face.
I take a peek and see you smile.
I am yours.
I close my eyes for another taste,
it so sweet.
I follow the trace,
I am yours.

Mint

A cool breath rushes
A tint of sweetness
A fresh scent
It feels like a new beginning
Its taste so unique
Mint
It is there for you
when times are tense
You don't know if you should
Mint
Cool, sweet, fresh
A kiss
I found a mint
but not what you may think
She makes me feel just the same
Just like a cool breath
It passed so quick
So here I wait
For a kiss

A dance

Why do we have memories?
Is it a place where we can escape
to the times of comfort?
Perhaps bring a smile to our face
remembering those good ol' days?
Maybe to revisit an old friend to ask
why they have gone?
Or is it to torture us?
Reminding us of times we once had
and cannot get back
To serve as a warning of love's treachery?
They say that love is patient
and that it is kind.
What they don't tell you is that
it is also uncomfortable and quite unknown
But as long as she keeps dancing
I will be there waiting to join.

Equinox

Behold, for the light rises over the horizon.
She reaches out beyond for you.
The morning dew glistening to a tune.
Death's curtains pulled back to show what's in
bloom.
She holds you to illuminate the day
the heart blossoms reborn from decay.
You have risen, forged anew.
Behold my child for I have you.

Paradox

Love is surely patient and kind.
But it is also painful and destructive
A contradiction of humanity, are we doomed to
fail?
Why is it that someone that brings you so much
joy, can also be the very thing that withers you
away.
Even the Christ, through his love, faced the
greatest pain and punishment for it.
Is love death in disguise?
Though death does lead to life so maybe it is
love.
But does that mean that life is fleeting, maybe
worthless?
But how is that possible?
For without it you cannot have death.
Is life love too? A contradiction.
Illogical, a cosmic idea beyond our
understanding yet we have to live every day.

The Word

A word divine
but the self is mine
A reality forms to define
Beauty in simplicity
Life in complexity
Suffering in longevity
Death is depravity
White flowers bloom
A lover faces doom
A reality defined
Turn the page
Cannot comprehend
The End.

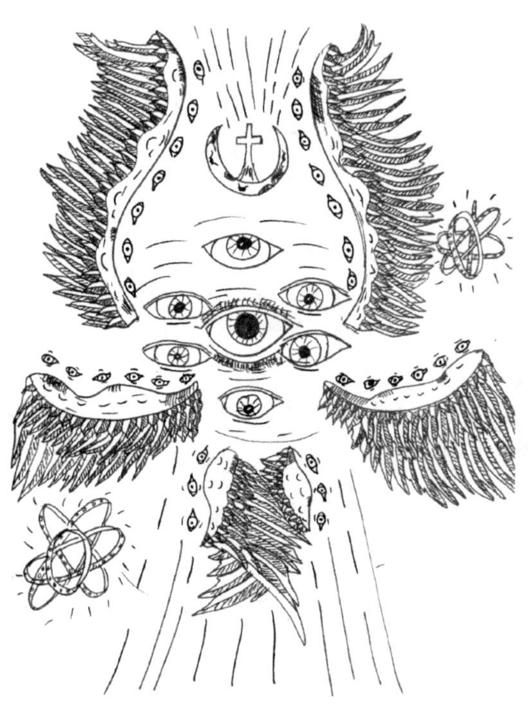

An ancient hymn

Why does the heart sing its hymn?
When the spear pierces its limb
A grim tale from our sins
And here begins, the motion from within.
A heart that knows not pain
Until a sword called love makes sure it's slain.

Smoke

A hopeful smoke from a passion of before.
Coming from a kindling, I want to reignite
once more.
It came from a fire so great it kept us warm.
But as long as it does not rain
the heart will play the rhythm of the song
So that the smoke can keep dancing
in memory of that love once more.

Burden

The heart is a burden
that I did not ask to carry.
Though it is strong, it knows no bounds
And in its strife
It can take my will
But on this voyage of the unknown
This curse becomes a necessity
In pursuit of a love that once was known.
Where I discover its burden is my own.

Ballad

On this stage I dance alone
An audience of none to hear my song
but I am to play the drama nonetheless
Until death's curtain closes out the rest.
Even in the prowl of the night
one can still find a candle lit tonight.
And in its flicker she calls to me,
to dance one last time.
Beyond the curtain for the heart's divine.

Mind

The mind made of symmetry, it split in two
One seeks beauty while the other seeks to rule
Though they stand divided in love
The heart must stay united
For if it breaks they find no joy
The kingdom in my head lost in musing.
Suddenly, a touch from her
A sense forgotten
frees my soul
from the logic of this world.
I find myself again in the symmetry of the two.

Calling

The constant beating heart is a
maddening reminder it has no one.
Its beat, a song for no one, but silence to listen.
My heart like a caged beast ready to burst out of
my chest, no one to reclaim it. A battle for
meaning with no home to call my own
A gypsy of this world until
My Father calls me from my roam.

Breathe

A breath draws life
A breath reels us closer to death
In this reality of constant paradox
not even the mind can make it orthodox
So it is through the heart we search the logos
To find meaning in our being
But in our pursuit of the truth
We forget to breathe and join the archives in our
tomb.

Feel

A touch euphoric
a journey through the heart
walls crumbling at your presence.
A beauty that remains in my mind.
A voyage that ended all too soon
shipwrecked on my own.
Yearning for that touch once more
to dance out into the moonlight
like before.

Siren

I let a siren in
on my floating ark.
A place constructed from
a flickering light, a kingdom of rebirth
she sang a song so sweet.
I let a siren in.
Lost in the moonlight of her eyes
inside my walls she now resides.
A temple that bloomed from destruction.
Colored windows, an altar of the heart.
I let a siren in.
Her touch, succulent, her mystery divine
wandering the halls
no purpose yet found.
Yet in the temple
her stained-glass window is abound
I know not what to do with her
I pray her soul is found
I let a siren in.
Now I float alone in the vastness of the sea.

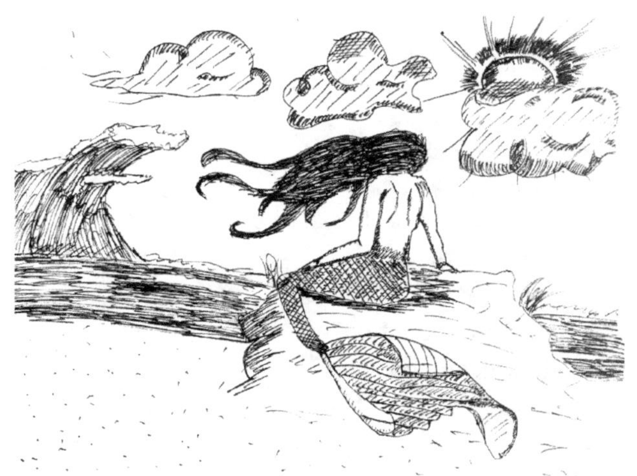

Beauty too

We stripped her of her garments
accusations of vanity.
We skinned her of beauty
cries of her seduction.
We bludgeoned out her mind
from pride's cowardice of her wisdom.
We broke off all her limbs
fearing of her justice.
We ripped out her heart
overwhelmed by love.
Now we sit in darkness
dreaming of her light.
Floating in a void, no purpose to pursue.
Even though she lay as a corpse
her spirit sits serene in chaos.
As the fools wither from her absence
she waits for our return in the mercy of her arms.

Waves

Crushing waves across the horizon
disorientation of the rocking vessel.
The storm is brewing
A darkness in the sky,
Lightning shrieks
The stone daggers of the sea cut out into the
soul.
The storm is brewing.
A woman robed in glory points.

In the chaos her beauty provides direction.
A familiar siren's song through the storm.
In just a moment the jaws of the leviathan crush
my journey.
I float into the wet abyss.
Awaiting for a siren's song to join,
In the hymn of her robed glory.

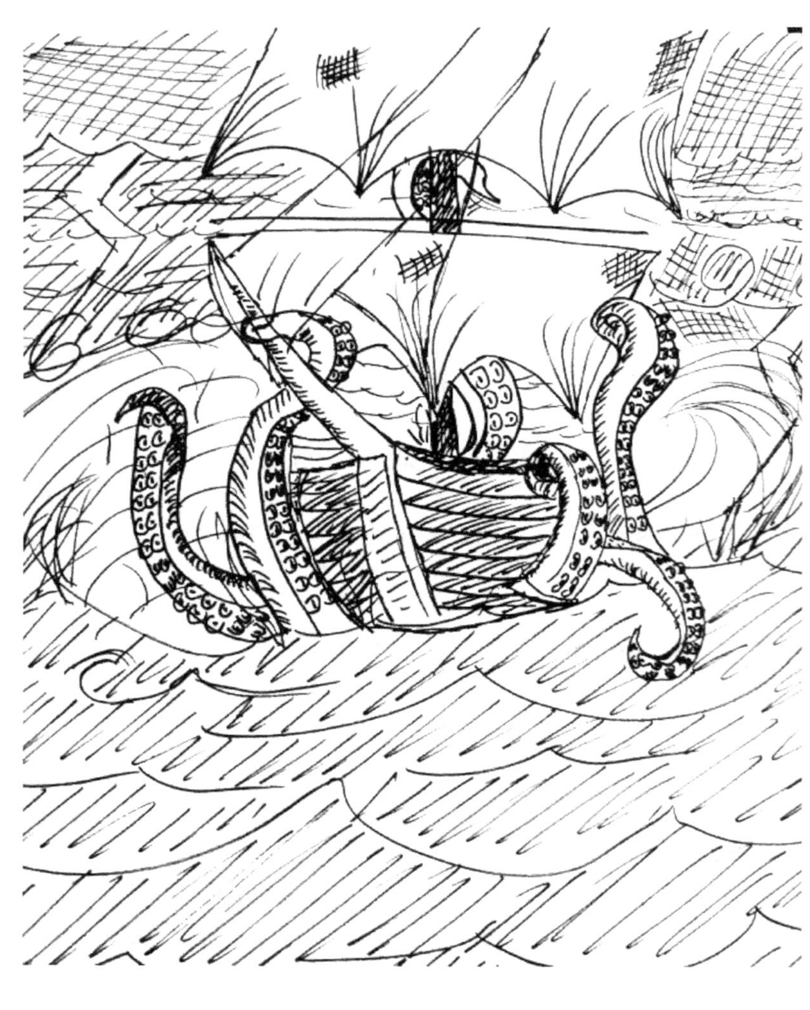

www.ingramcontent.com/pod-product-compliance
Lightning Source LLC
LaVergne TN
LVHW051248200726
843510LV00011B/1738